THE MONKS' DORMITORY was a long aisled building on two floors.

THE INFIRMARY was where the sick and infirm monks were looked after. The remains, which now lie beneath the school playing fields can only be seen as outlines from the air.

THE CHAPTER HOUSE was where the main business of the Abbey was carried out. Only the doorway can now be seen. It was also used as a main burial place for some of the abbots.

THE CRYPT formed a basement below the High Altar, and was used both for worship and for burials. Some 14th-century wall paintings can still be seen on the left-hand wall.

THE CHAPEL OF ST PANCRAS is the most eastern of the line of original Anglo-Saxon churches probably built during the 7th century. It survived the major Norman rebuilding and the surviving east wall and chancel were rebuilt during the late 14th century.

THE LADY CHAPEL is the crypt of an early 15th-century chapel, rebuilt later in the 15th century. It was probably intended for the special performances of masses for Our Lady.

THE CAMPANILE MOUND is so called because a bell tower or campanile once stood here. It was probably built of timber with stone foundations in the 15th century.

ST AUGUSTINE'S ABBEY
Canterbury

THIS ABBEY, *founded by St Augustine in around 598, is one of the oldest monastic sites in the country. It was built to mark the success of the evangelical mission sent by Pope Gregory the Great to reintroduce Christianity to the south of England. The Abbey was used initially as the burial place for the kings of Kent and the early archbishops of Canterbury.*

After the Norman Conquest, in the eleventh century, it became, and took on the appearance of, a standard Benedictine Abbey. It continued in religious use until 1538, when, like all other monasteries in the country, it was suppressed by Henry VIII as part of the Dissolution of the Monasteries.

After the Dissolution, part of the site was converted into a royal palace by Henry VIII, and was used as a resting place for royal journeys from London to the south-east ports.

Evidence of all these phases of the site's history can still be seen. This guidebook provides a history of the site, and a tour, based on information gathered from the remains of the buildings, excavation evidence and documentary sources.

ABOVE: *A particularly striking medieval tile found at St Augustine's showing a human face and torso with tunic and pelleted belt (probably a monk)*

2

HISTORY
of the Site

DESCRIPTION OF THE SITE

The site of St Augustine's Abbey lies just outside the Roman and (later) medieval city walls, on the main road east out of Canterbury to the coast.

It is likely that the original land granted to Augustine by King Ethelbert of Kent for the foundation of the monastery was part of a royal estate on the edge of the early Saxon settlement. This probably included the site of St Martin's church which, together with the surrounding estate, was later to be the property of the archbishop.

The precinct, covering an area of approximately 12 hectares (30 acres), can still largely be traced on the ground today. The monastery also owned the manor of Longport adjacent to the precinct, with the home farm at Barton Court to supply its immediate needs.

When the monastery was dissolved, the abbey precinct had a series of individual owners until 1791, when parts of it were sold as separate plots. In 1848 St Augustine's Missionary College was founded on part of the site. This marked the start of attempts to preserve the site, and a series of excavations carried out since 1900 have revealed the remains of most of the main buildings.

The area now in the care of English Heritage represents only a part of the precinct, covering the area of the main cloister buildings, but excluding the Abbot's lodging, the main gates, the infirmary, and the outer court which contained most of the later domestic and service buildings.

Parts of the monastic precinct are now occupied by the nineteenth-century buildings of the King's School (formerly St Augustine's College), the more modern buildings of Christ Church College, and Canterbury prison.

THE ARRIVAL OF ST AUGUSTINE: THE RE-INTRODUCTION OF CHRISTIANITY

A monastery was founded on this site in about 598 by Augustine with a small group of monks, who had been sent from Rome by Pope Gregory the Great to restore Christianity to southern England.

Christianity had first been introduced to England by the Romans, but with the collapse of the Roman Empire, and increasing invasions by pagan peoples from northern Europe (Angles, Saxons and Jutes, soon to be known as the English), the Christian faith survived only in the unconquered Celtic regions of Wales and the west.

England at this time was divided into a number of separate kingdoms. Augustine aimed to convert the royal families, hoping that the general population would then follow their example.

Kent was chosen as the landing place for the mission, as it was the kingdom of Ethelbert, one of the most powerful leaders of his time. His wife, Bertha, was a Frankish princess and already a practising Christian. It is thought that the royal palace was located just to the east of

OPPOSITE: *Pope Gregory sending St Augustine to England to convert the people to Christianity, from a mid-eleventh-century German missal*

BODLEIAN LIBRARY Ms Fell f 45r

An initial from a twelfth-century English manuscript showing St Augustine and King Ethelbert of Kent

A comb traditionally thought to have been a gift from Pope Gregory to Queen Bertha

BELOW: *St Benedict in an eleventh-century illustration from Canterbury Cathedral Priory. The inscription on the saint's halo refers to him as the father of the monks. The monks at St Augustine's based their daily lives around the rules laid out by St Benedict*

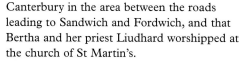

Canterbury in the area between the roads leading to Sandwich and Fordwich, and that Bertha and her priest Liudhard worshipped at the church of St Martin's.

The missionaries probably arrived in 597 and were welcomed by Ethelbert. They were given accommodation and the freedom to preach to his people, although it was probably not until later that year that Ethelbert himself was converted to the Christian faith.

The conversion of the King marked a turning point in the success of the mission. As a result Augustine was given an old Roman church in Canterbury which was to become his cathedral, dedicated to Christ the Saviour (Christ Church), and a site to the east of the city to found a monastery.

THE BUILDING OF THE ANGLO-SAXON MONASTERY

The new monastery had a number of functions. It was used as accommodation for the monks who had accompanied Augustine from Italy. It also acted as a special burial place for the kings and archbishops, which, following imperial Roman tradition, had to be outside the city walls.

At first Augustine must have acted both as archbishop of the new diocese and as head of the new community. However, when the monastery was built, Peter, one of Augustine's original companions, was elected as the first abbot.

Information about the early development of the monastery is limited, but comes both from documentary sources (particularly the work of Bede written in the eighth century) and evidence uncovered by archaeological excavations.

The Abbey must have included domestic buildings such as a dining hall and a dormitory, as well as a series of chapels for worship. Very little is known about the domestic quarters, although earlier buildings on a slightly different alignment, but of unknown date, have been uncovered by excavations below some of the later medieval buildings.

More information is available about the churches. We know that Augustine built a number of separate chapels in a line, similar to ones he had seen on the Continent.

LIFE IN THE ANGLO-SAXON MONASTERY

Links with the Italian church and with Pope Gregory were strongly maintained at first. The first six abbots of the new monastery were all Italian, either from the initial band of missionaries who had arrived with Augustine, or from a group sent by Pope Gregory in 601 to help with the introduction of the new faith in England. The monks probably continued to base their daily lives on the Rule of St Benedict, as they had in their Italian houses. Pope Gregory continued to support the mission by sending gifts of vestments, gold and silver altar vessels, relics and books.

Life in the Saxon monastery revolved around the daily services with chanted recitals from the Book of Psalms. The Rule of St Benedict also recommended that time should be allowed for study and manual labour. Before the formation of universities during the twelfth century, monasteries were the only centres for higher education in England.

EDUCATION AND THE MONASTIC LIBRARY

During the time of Abbot Hadrian (669–706) and Archbishop Theodore (668–690) the church school at Canterbury was noted for its teaching, and attracted scholars from all over England.

It is not clear whether the school was located at the cathedral or the abbey, but it seems that monks and clerics from both communities were involved. A wide range of subjects were taught including scripture, poetry, law, calligraphy, astronomy, music and medicine. Monks at this time were well educated, some having entered the monastery as children. During the seventh and eighth centuries, before the organisation of the abbeys became more complex, even abbots had time to produce manuscripts.

Little is known about the educational life of the Abbey during the ninth century, but there seems to have been a revival in the production of manuscripts after Dunstan's reforms of the

An illustration of St Luke from a Bible sent over to St Augustine's Abbey by Pope Gregory

Detail from an eleventh-century book on plants produced at St Augustine's

tenth century. A number of early eleventh-century manuscripts which were produced at St Augustine's still survive, and it appears that the scriptorium flourished in the years before the Norman Conquest.

By the time Abbot Scolland arrived at the Abbey in 1070, St Augustine's had an extensive library. The first books were brought over from Italy by Augustine himself, and others were sent by Pope Gregory, one of which still survives in Corpus Christi College, Cambridge. It seems likely that they would have included works of both a religious and secular nature. Abbot Scolland had been involved in copying manuscripts at his abbey of Mont St Michel, and brought a number of books with him, including those which reflected his interests in history and medicine.

A page from a catalogue of the books in the library at St Augustine's Abbey in the late fifteenth century

RIGHT: *A page from a book on plants and their properties produced by a monk of St Augustine's Abbey in the late eleventh century*

FAR RIGHT: *Part of a picture showing St Dunstan in devotion to Christ. Dunstan was the most important figure in the monastic revival of the tenth century. He may have drawn this picture himself*

In the two centuries following the Norman Conquest the production of illuminated manuscripts flourished, although by the late twelfth century it is likely that most were produced by lay scribes rather than by monks. Some monks had the opportunity to develop their own academic interests, and sometimes gave books to the monastic library, as in the case of Adam, who was Sub-Prior of the Abbey in the early thirteenth century.

A late fifteenth-century catalogue of books in the St Augustine's library survives, and indicates that by this date it housed almost 2000 volumes.

After the writings of Bede, we have very little evidence about life in the Abbey during the ninth and tenth centuries, although it seems likely that the routine of monastic life continued without major incident. During the ninth century, increasing numbers of Viking raids threatened the security of many monastic communities, particularly those near the coast. However, though Canterbury did suffer from Danish invasions, it seems that the Abbey was not particularly affected.

MONASTIC REFORM UNDER DUNSTAN

In the middle of the tenth century monasticism underwent a revival both in continental Europe and across England. In England this was largely due to the influence of the monk Dunstan with the help of Oswald and King Ethelwold.

Dunstan was an educated monk with royal connections, and in 940 he was elected Abbot of Glastonbury. Under Dunstan the Abbey was reorganised, and became renowned as a centre of learning. In 959 he became Archbishop of Canterbury, and proceeded to reorganise and reform the cathedral on monastic lines. At this time St Augustine's also came under the influence of the reform movement and was ruled for about thirty years by abbots who supported Dunstan's ideals.

In 970 the abbots of the reformed monasteries met and drew up a document known as the *Regularis Concordia* which agreed a common approach to daily monastic life. It placed emphasis on the performance of elaborate rituals and formal periods of communal prayer.

At St Augustine's this period of spiritual revival was also marked by a number of additions and alterations to the existing buildings. The church of St Peter and St Paul was enlarged by the demolition of the west wall and the extension of the nave over the original western end. New structures were then added including, possibly, a cemetery chapel some distance to the west of the original church. The church of St Peter and St Paul was rededicated by Archbishop Dunstan in 978 to St Augustine as well as St Peter and St Paul and the Abbey became known as St Augustine's.

THE LATE SAXON PERIOD

After Dunstan's reforms, the domestic buildings at St Augustine's were probably rebuilt to bring them more in line with the standard layout of the new Benedictine houses.

Documentary evidence suggests that a cloister was built by Abbot Aelfmaer (1006–17), although archaeological evidence points to at least two phases of building below the present cloister. Unfortunately no dating evidence was found during the excavation of these structures.

More extensive alterations were made to the churches under Abbot Wulfric II (1047–59). In 1047 he paid for the completion of a tower. Its precise location is not identified, but it may correspond to a massive foundation uncovered in excavations during the 1950s at the west end of the later Norman church. This foundation belonged to a free-standing structure to the west of the existing Anglo-Saxon churches. A further small chapel with a curved western end (apse), and a slightly later circular tower at the west end, also seem to date from the eleventh century.

The main project undertaken by Abbot Wulfric, however, was the provision of an octagonal building or rotunda to link the existing church of St Peter and St Paul with the chapel of St Mary. Wulfric may have been inspired by structures seen on a trip to Rheims in France. A similar structure is shown in an illuminated manuscript produced at the Abbey at the time (right). The construction of the rotunda involved the demolition of the east end of the church of St Peter and St Paul, and the west end of St Mary's, together with the removal of the shrine of St Mildred and other sacred relics. It seems unlikely that the rotunda was ever completed, as Abbot Wulfric died in 1059 and his successor, Abbot Scolland, replanned the entire church.

ABOVE: *An illustration copied from Aelfric's* Anglo-Saxon Paraphrases of the Old Testament *by a monk at St Augustine's in about 1050. It shows workmen building a tower which is not unlike what we know of the rotunda built by Abbot Wulfric at St Augustine's in the eleventh century*

The churches and cloister in the mid-eleventh century, showing how the early churches were to be joined together by a rotunda (drawing by Peter Urmston based on an earlier drawing by Terry Ball)

THE NORMAN REBUILDING

T he Norman Conquest had a profound impact on the organisation of the church, as well as the general spread of monasticism throughout England.

William I maintained his authority and upheld his claim to the English throne by providing his supporters with lands and titles and by reviving the rule of religion. He appointed his own nominees to key positions within the church organisation, and encouraged the establishment of new monasteries and the rebuilding of existing foundations.

In 1070, Lanfranc, an Italian monk who had been influential in the development of the Norman abbeys of Caen and Bec, was made Archbishop of Canterbury. Scolland, a monk from Mont St Michel in Normandy, was appointed Abbot of St Augustine's. Lanfranc proceeded to reorganise the cathedral clergy, and to bring the lives of monks in existing religious foundations into line with practices on the continent.

A Norman foot soldier on his way to do battle at Hastings (from the Bayeux Tapestry)

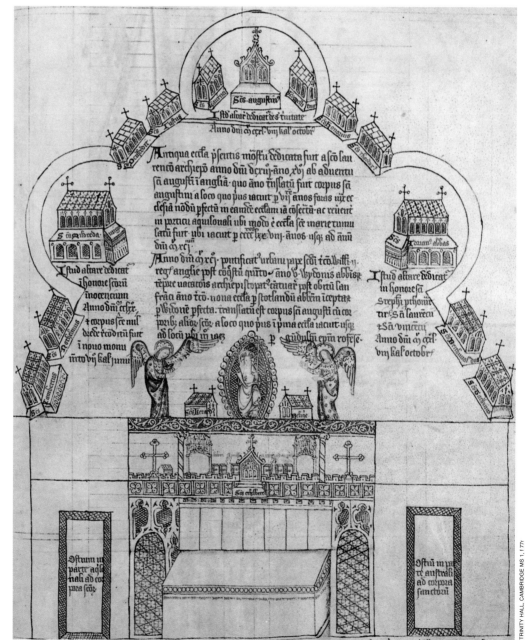

The drawing of the new presbytery built in the late eleventh century is from a book produced in 1414 by a monk of St Augustine's called Thomas of Elmham. It gives us a good idea of how the shrines were laid out

Some monks resented the Norman seizure of power, and the impact it had on their religious traditions, but most new abbots seem to have been accepted by their monastic communities.

At the time of Abbot Scolland's arrival, the Abbey consisted of a series of buildings which had been extended piecemeal over the years, with some parts of the churches dating back to the seventh century. The abbey chronicle of this time records that Scolland was 'frightened by the danger that the old monastery, consumed by long decay, might collapse', and he therefore discussed plans with the Pope, Alexander II, for a major rebuilding programme. The rebuilding of the church in the Norman, Romanesque style began almost immediately, and was completed by the succeeding abbots Wydo (1087–99) and Hugh of Fleury (1099–1124). Work on the domestic ranges, laid out around a cloister, seems to have proceeded after the main work on the church.

We have considerable evidence of how the church was constructed, and the people involved. This is thanks to Goscelin, a well-known historian, employed by the Abbey to write about the grand ceremonies, called 'translations', which took place when the relics of the early archbishops were moved into the new church.

The building work was carried out under the overall supervision of a master mason named Blither. He was described by Goscelin as 'the most eminent master of the craftsmen'. Large quantities of stone were imported from quarries on the Isle of Wight and from Caen and Marquise in France. It was transported by ships which may have belonged to the Abbey.

Work on the new church began at the east end with the removal of the relics of the Kentish kings followed by demolition of the chapel of St Mary and the partially constructed rotunda. On the site of St Mary's, a new crypt was built (see page 22) with the presbytery above, to house the high altar, and a place for shrines of the saints. These formed an apsidal

(semi-circular) east end with three semi-circular chapels at each level, and would have been similar to buildings in France familiar to Abbot Scolland. To the west of the presbytery was the monks' choir, with apsidal north and south transepts forming the cross arms of the church. These, together with the foundations of the nave, were probably built before Abbot Scolland died in 1087.

Scolland's successor, Abbot Wydo, was chosen by the Archbishop of Canterbury rather than the monks. This caused considerable discontent at the Abbey. The opposing monks were removed and about twenty monks from Christ Church were introduced to replace them.

The demolition of the church of St Peter and St Paul and the ceremonial removal of the remains of the old archbishops in 1091, were carried out under Abbot Wydo, who built a central tower over the choir. He then completed the nave, and possibly laid the foundations for the two towers at the west end of the church. The church was probably finally completed by the next abbot, Hugh of Fleury. The towers were highly decorated, with elaborate blind arcading, columns and arches.

The interior of the church was also highly decorated, with painted carvings of animals and foliage. A large amount of carved stonework has been recovered during clearance, although the original position of much of this is unknown.

After the completion of the church, attention moved to the up-dating of the domestic quarters. This involved a gradual replacement of the original Saxon buildings over a number of years. By the end of the twelfth century the main ranges around the cloister were complete.

LEFT: *A stone corbel carved with a grotesque figure and inscribed 'Robertus me fecit' (Robertus made me)*

ABOVE: *A drawing of a Caen stone segment of a door arch carved with a dragon from around 1170*

Fragment of one of a number of voussoir stones with some surviving paintwork, that formed part of an arch found during excavations in 1975

THE MEDIEVAL MONASTERY

Benedictine monks worshipping together at Mass – the Benedictine routine consisted of eight church services each day

Henry VIII depicted in an initial letter from the Valor Ecclesiasticus, *the document containing the valuation of all church property ordered by Cromwell in 1535*

Life in the medieval Abbey of St Augustine's continued the patterns of daily life established by the Saxon and Norman monks. The main purpose of a monk's life was the worship of God.

However, with the increasingly complex organisation of the Abbey, the number of monks holding an official position must have increased. A custumal, a book setting out an intricate code of customs for community life in the Abbey, survives from this period. It gives an insight into the use of the various buildings and the forms of religious ritual used here. The thirteenth century saw the completion of the rebuilding of the church after a fire of 1168. Although it kept its basic Norman appearance, there was a tendency for fixtures and fittings to become more elaborate. The shrine of St Augustine was rebuilt in 1220, the High Altar rededicated in 1240, and the choir stalls replaced in 1292.

The buildings around the cloister were also substantially rebuilt in this period, and towards the end of the thirteenth century there can have been few occasions when work was not being carried out somewhere on the site. The general picture given by the documented building work at this time is of increasing comfort in the domestic quarters. The Prior was given separate chambers in 1267, and in 1276 the cloisters were improved with the addition of columns and a roof. During the 1270s repairs to the infirmary included the addition of a *misericord* (a room where meat could be eaten), indicating that it was becoming more usual for the monks to eat meat. The refectory, kitchen, brewhouse and bakehouse were also rebuilt.

Beyond the main cloister area the Great Court was enlarged, a new gatehouse constructed, and a base or outer court added to the north. This area contained buildings associated with the running of the Abbey's extensive estates, and included a new cellarer's range, bakehouse, brewhouse and barns for the storage of grain.

The fourteenth century saw a continuation of building activity, although the projects undertaken were generally smaller in scale. The chapter house was rebuilt, and further chapels were added to the church. An earthquake in 1382 led to repairs and the upgrading of several buildings including the west window of the church, and the addition of a number of bells.

During the fifteenth century, building work at the Abbey slowed down, possibly because of the Abbey's considerable debts.

THE MONASTIC ESTATES

From the beginning of monasticism it was intended that an abbey should be as self-sufficient as possible and therefore it needed land. Although in the early days it was expected that monks would do some manual labour, it was anticipated that most of this would be done by servants. As monastic organisations became more complex, it was necessary to generate a substantial income to pay for the upkeep of the community. Much of the land was given to the abbey by rich benefactors in exchange for the saying of prayers, but some was bought on the open market.

St Augustine's developed extensive estates mostly in East Kent. The land close to the Abbey was probably given by King Ethelbert, and large areas in Thanet were given by King Cnut. Although early benefactors were generally members of the royal household, grants of land were also made by noblemen. All the land was granted to St Augustine, patron and protector of the Abbey. Most of the lands were acquired either in the Saxon or early Norman period, but were often confirmed as belonging to the Abbey at later dates. At its height St Augustine's held almost 12,000 acres of land.

THE FINAL YEARS OF THE ABBEY AND THE DISSOLUTION

In 1522 John Essex or Foche was elected as the last abbot of St Augustine's. During his term in office, there was radical reform of the English church, and the demise of the monastic system in England.

In 1532, Henry VIII declared himself the Supreme Head of the Church of England and during the next few years there was increasing pressure for the reform or destruction of monastic institutions.

In 1535 Thomas Cromwell, Henry's Chief Minister, organised a survey of all church property and income as the basis for a tax assessment, known as the *Valor Ecclesiasticus*. This was accompanied by a visit to all monasteries to identify those houses where there was slackness of religious observance.

In 1536 the majority of the minor monastic houses, and those with an annual income of less than £200, were closed down. St Augustine's Abbey was finally the victim of a second series of visitations organised by Cromwell in 1538 which resulted in the closure of all the remaining larger abbeys.

St Augustine's was surrendered to the King's Commissioners on 30 July 1538 by Abbot John Essex and the thirty remaining monks, ending the continuous use of the site for religious purposes for just over 940 years.

The Abbot and the monks were given a pension. The Abbot was also allowed a manor house to live in, but the monks usually had to supplement their pensions by doing other jobs. Many became parish priests.

After the surrender of the monastery, its treasures, such as the books and the gold and silver plate, were scattered. Of the 2000 volumes listed in a fifteenth-century catalogue of the St Augustine's library, about 200 survive today, and a sixteenth-century, silver-mounted coconut cup is all that survives of the plate. This is now in the Cathedral treasury.

LEFT: *The Coconut Cup – the grace cup of Abbot Foche – was passed down through the family of the last abbot*

BELOW: *A reconstruction drawing of the Abbey in about 1500 – a few years before its closure – giving a good impression of its scale (drawing by Terry Ball)*

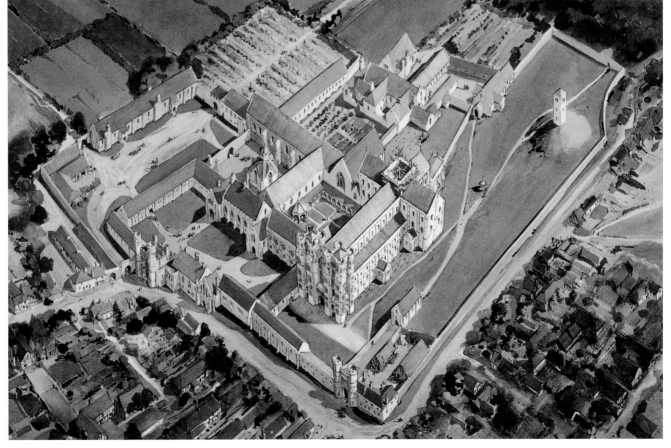

Two medieval glazed ceramic floor tiles found at St Augustine's Abbey. Above: design of a lion passant and below: one of a four-tile pattern showing foetal animals in a cusped border

Abbots in a House of Lords procession in 1512, including abbots (from left to right) of Glastonbury, Bury St Edmunds, St Augustine's at Canterbury and St Albans

INFLUENTIAL ABBOTS OF ST AUGUSTINE'S

The Abbot was the father of the house, and was responsible for the spiritual and financial well-being of the abbey. A total of 72 abbots of St Augustine's Abbey have been recorded, although little is known about many of them. Peter was the first abbot, and was one of the original Italian monks who accompanied St Augustine from Rome. The other abbots listed here are those mentioned in the text of this guidebook.

Abbot Peter (598–607)

Abbot Hadrian (669–706)

Abbot Aelfmar (1006–1017)

Abbot Scolland (1070–1087)

Abbot Wulfric II (1047–1059)

Abbot Wydo (1087–1099)

Abbot Hugh of Fleury (1099–1124)

Abbot Roger of Chichester (1253–1273)

Abbot Fyndon (1283–1309)

Abbot Thomas Pouncy (1334–1343)

Abbot Dunster (1486–1496)

Abbot John Dygon (1497–1509)

Abbot John Essex or Foche (1522–1538)

✠ ✠ ✠

CHRONICLERS

The history of the Abbey was documented by a number of chroniclers, and from their writing comes most of our information about monastic events.

BEDE (673–735): Was a monk at the monastery of Jarrow in the kingdom of Northumbria from the age of seven. In his own words his "chief delight has always been in study, teaching and writing". He became the most famous historical writer of his times, and wrote *The History of the English Church and People* which tells the story of the Anglo-Saxons from their arrival in England until his own time.

GOSCELIN was a French monk from St Bertin, who came to England with Hereman, Bishop of Salisbury, in 1058. He seems to have served as a monk both at Ely and Ramsey, before moving to St Augustine's towards the end of the eleventh century. He had a reputation as a writer and reviser of saints' lives as well as being a composer. He was brought to St Augustine's to write about the solemn ceremonies called translations that took place when the saints were moved

into the new church, and probably also wrote the music to mark these celebrations. He also wrote a popular account of the *Life and Miracles of St Augustine*.

THOMAS SPROTT was a monk at the abbey during the early part of the thirteenth century and wrote a chronicle including the early history of the Abbey from the Creation through to 1232. This document seems to have been lost by the early eighteenth century, but was used as the main source by the other medieval chroniclers.

WILLIAM THORNE: The early part of his chronicle copied the information from Thomas Sprott, although he added to it from other sources. This continues the history of the Abbey up to the reign of Richard II with the last entry dating to 1397.

THOMAS OF ELMHAM: Was a monk of St Augustine's in the early fifteenth century, and held the office of treasurer in 1407. He ceased to be a Benedictine monk in 1414 when he joined the Cluniac Order, and became the Prior of Lenton in Nottinghamshire.

A miniature of Henry VIII's fourth wife, Anne of Cleves, by the early sixteenth-century artist Holbein. Henry VIII sent Holbein abroad to paint prospective brides and bring back the pictures to show him

THE CREATION OF A ROYAL PALACE

Unlike many monastic houses which were leased or sold to large local landowners or royal favourites, St Augustine's was retained in Crown hands.

In 1539 Henry VIII converted some buildings into a royal residence in preparation for the arrival of the new Queen, his fourth wife Anne of Cleves. This also fitted into a wider scheme of establishing stopping-places for the King on journeys between London and the Cinque Ports.

The palace was largely converted from the buildings of the Great Court, notably the abbot's lodging, although some demolition and rebuilding was also required. The work was carried out under the direction of James Needham, the Surveyor of the King's Works, and it is from his detailed accounts that the sequence of building is known. The main phase of work seems to have been carried out rather rapidly between the beginning of October and the end of December 1539, with as many as 350 craftsmen being employed on the site.

The existing buildings of the abbot's lodging were converted to form accommodation for the King and his chaplain together with a hall for guests. The main new building work was to provide accommodation for Anne of Cleves and involved the demolition of some old lodgings probably on the south side of the Great Court.

DEMOLITION OF THE ABBEY AND LATER USES

The building works were completed for the arrival of Anne of Cleves, and Henry VIII is known to have stayed at the palace on a number of subsequent occasions. In 1541 he gave orders for the church to be dismantled. The lead from the roof was melted down and sold to provide cash for the Treasury, and much of the stonework was sent to France for the building of the fortifications of Calais. The demolition of the church and other monastic buildings seems to have taken a number of years, and records show that materials were still being sold to local people twenty years later. The site was gradually reduced to its foundations, except for the north wall of the nave and the Ethelbert Tower, which formed the southern wall of the new palace.

After the reign of Henry VIII, the palace was not much used, and was leased to a succession of noble families — initially to Lord Cobham, and, by 1612, to Lord and Lady Wotton. A number of royal visits are recorded — Queen Elizabeth I visited in 1573, and Charles I in 1625 — but generally little interest was shown in the property.

Although the King's palace and privy garden were separated from the rest of the site by a wall which can still be seen, the whole of the monastic precinct seems to have been leased out. During the tenancy of Lord and Lady Wotton, formal gardens were laid out by John Tradescant the Elder, the famous gardener.

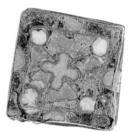

A medieval gold cloisonné plate with colourful enamelling found at St Augustine's. It was probably a mount for a ring

A painting of the ruined Ethelbert Tower by John Bulman (c. 1780)

A depiction of Longport by John Bulman showing the eighteenth-century hospital building

In 1659 the site passed to the Hales family who retained it until the early nineteenth century. In 1692 Canterbury was affected by an earthquake which damaged the Ethelbert Tower and possibly the palace buildings. It is likely that the gardens also disappeared at this time.

By the 1770s some of the buildings of the old palace were in use as a brewery, maltings, and public house, with the courtyard being used as a bowling green and skittle alley. The area where the formal gardens had been was now leased as grazing land, with a farmhouse built into the surviving ruins of St Pancras.

Towards the end of the eighteenth century the Hales family started to sell off parts of the monastic precinct. In 1791 the south-eastern parts of the site were sold for the construction of the Canterbury Gaol and the building of the Kent and Canterbury Hospital (1793). When the hospital was being built in the 1790s, a number of burials, some of them in lead or stone coffins, were uncovered by the workmen. This is the first record of items from the Abbey being found through excavation.

In 1801 Hasted, the local Kent historian wrote: "... *in opening the cemetery they found a stone coffin of one block with a cover, having a ridge running along its middle, and containing a skeleton, wrapt in a coarse woolen cloth, tied or gathered at the hands and feet, which bore handling very well, but was easily torn. The bones were entire, the hair red, curled, strong and elastic, and about two inches long; under the head was a hollow stone like a pillow.*"

After the death of Sir Edward Hales in 1804, the rest of the precinct was sold off in lots. In

A painting of A. J. Beresford Hope who bought the site of St Augustine's Abbey in 1844, built a missionary college and encouraged excavations and the preservation of the ruins

1826, William Beer became sole owner of the St Augustine's Brewery. Trade flourished, and in 1836 extensive improvements were made to the gardens, which were opened to the public as pleasure grounds.

REVIVAL OF INTEREST: THE BUILDING OF ST AUGUSTINE'S COLLEGE

B y the end of the eighteenth century the site of St Augustine's Abbey had almost been forgotten. Despite the growth of interest in monastic sites, and the artistic taste for engravings of romantic ruins, little of the monastic buildings survived to provide a focus for the site. Most of the artistic representations of the ruins are of the Ethelbert Tower, which stood almost complete until 1822.

The use of part of the area as a brewery and inn was increasingly seen as inappropriate, and in 1844 A. J. Beresford Hope bought the site when it came up for sale. Shortly after its purchase, the architect William Butterfield was employed to restore the medieval buildings which were hidden under the eighteenth-century facade of the brewery. It was suggested that this part of the site might be used for some

religious purpose, and by 1848 a missionary college had been established. St Augustine's College remained here until 1947, and established the St Augustine's Foundation which was dedicated to recovering the monastic precinct to enable excavation and the preservation of the ruins.

The buildings of the missionary college are now occupied by the King's School. The main body of the site was placed in State guardianship in 1938, with further land being included in 1941 and 1960. The southern part of the precinct, formerly occupied by the hospital, was included as part of the site when the hospital was demolished in 1974. The area of public gardens was incorporated in 1996. The whole of the southern part of the monastic precinct, including the buildings around the cloister, is now managed by English Heritage.

St Augustine's Abbey, together with St Martin's Church and the Cathedral, was designated a World Heritage site by UNESCO in 1989.

St Martin's Church, Canterbury, where Queen Bertha is thought to have worshipped. It is now part of the World Heritage Site

A depiction of the internal quadrangle at St Augustine's College, Canterbury in the mid-nineteenth century, by L. L. Razé

TOUR
of the Abbey

ou enter the Abbey grounds through the museum. In medieval times a visitor would have entered by one of the gatehouses, as, by the thirteenth century, the monastery was enclosed by a high precinct wall. Two of the medieval gatehouses can still be viewed from the outside, although they are now privately owned and therefore not part of the tour. These are the gate to the cemetery and the main gate rebuilt by Abbot Fyndon in the early fourteenth century. After exploring the site, you could turn right out of the museum and walk round the outside of the wall into Monastery Street to see these impressive gates.

The recently built museum incorporates an exhibition about the Abbey displaying stones and artefacts discovered on the site. The site of the museum was that of the medieval cemetery. This was used for burials by those city parish churches that did not have their own cemetery.

The site of St Augustine's Abbey presents a challenge to the visitor, as, apart from the north wall of the nave ahead of you, and the chapel of St Pancras, few of the buildings survive to anything like their original height. It is therefore very difficult to imagine that the church was once only slightly smaller than Canterbury Cathedral, which can be glimpsed beyond the school to the west of St Augustine's.

Further confusion is caused by the fact that St Augustine's has the remains of not one, but two abbey complexes dating from different periods. The earlier Saxon monastery (see page 24) was largely replaced by more modern buildings shortly after the Norman Conquest of

1066. Some of the foundations of the Saxon structures were preserved below the later buildings, and have now in some places been exposed by excavations earlier this century, so the remains of both can be seen.

Before you go too far into the site, take the opportunity to look around.

Until 1972 the buildings of the late eighteenth-century County hospital still stood to the south of the monastic church.

The site as you see it is the result of careful archaeological excavations carried out over the last century, exposing the remains of the Abbey which had largely been lost from view.

To your left and in front of you are the buildings which now form part of the King's School, but which were originally part of the nineteenth-century St Augustine's Missionary College. These buildings are not open to the public, but can be viewed externally from Monastery Street which forms the boundary of the monastic precinct. In the medieval period, the main guest rooms for visitors to the Abbey were in this area. The existing buildings within the Great Court were largely designed by the architect William Butterfield during the 1840s.

When the monastery was dissolved in 1538, this area of the site was converted into a royal palace for Anne of Cleves. This has now largely disappeared, except for the brickwork at the top of the nave north wall in front of you, and the stone blocking in the Ethelbert Tower, which formed the exterior wall of the palace. On the other side of the wall to your left was the King's privy garden.

The main gateway to the Abbey in the Middle Ages, sometimes called Fyndon's Gate because it was rebuilt by Abbot Fyndon in the early fourteenth century

OPPOSITE: *The north wall of the nave of the Abbey church from the south-west and, on the bottom left of the picture, part of the ruined Ethelbert Tower*

THE CHURCH

Two standing stones placed near the present-day entrance to the Abbey site in the 1960s. They are not made of local stone and their true origin remains a mystery

The best-preserved building of St Augustine's is the monastic church. The church was the most important building of the monastery, where the monks would have maintained a daily round of services and heard Mass.

It is now difficult to imagine that the remains in front of you were part of a large Norman church, with a long nave, transepts, a central tower and an apsidal (rounded) east end. At the west end of the church the main entrance was flanked by highly decorative twin towers with intricately carved stonework.

The stone facing of the main walls (ashlar) has largely gone, having been sold off after the main buildings were demolished in the sixteenth century. Most of what you can now see is the rubble core of the walls.

WESTERN TOWERS
The original entrance to the church was through the west doorway (which now forms the boundary with King's School), but today access is through the site of the south-west tower.

The remains of the Ethelbert Tower, near the north nave wall

It is possible that some of the stonework of this tower is of late Anglo-Saxon date (early eleventh century) and belonged to a tower beside the gate to the forecourt of the Anglo-Saxon monastery. When the church was rebuilt during the Norman period, and the south-west tower was constructed, part of the earlier structure was retained and used as a buttress. It is likely that this tower was largely rebuilt after damage to the site by an earthquake in 1382.

STANDING STONES
Within the area of the tower you can see two large stones found during the excavation of the Anglo-Saxon churches. They were used in the foundations of the west wall of the vestibule. They were set up here in the 1960s and there has been considerable debate about their origin. They are not types of stone normally found in the Canterbury area, and must have either been carried by glaciers or deliberately brought to the area. Some people believe they may have formed part of a prehistoric monument, while others think that the larger stone was used by Augustine as a preaching cross. This will probably always be one of the mysteries of the site.

You are now standing at the west end of the monastic church, looking east towards the Chapel of St Pancras at the far end of the site. The monastic church was largely built under the first Norman abbot of the monastery, Abbot Scolland (1070–87), but was completed by the two succeeding abbots, Abbot Wydo (1087–99) and Abbot Hugh of Fleury (1099–1124).

The northernmost of the two towers, part of which you can still see, was partially destroyed in 1692 but remained standing until 1822. It became known as the Ethelbert Tower. Athough it was part of the original Norman building, it was altered during the fifteenth century. You can still see the remains of one of the original Romanesque capitals behind the later refaced wall.

THE NAVE
From here you can appreciate the size of the church. The nave was eleven bays in length, and was divided from the monks' choir and presbytery by a rood screen (see page 20). This area was used for worship by the ordinary people of Canterbury on special occasions.

The surviving north wall of the nave gives some idea of the height of the aisles, while the nave itself would have been even higher. The north aisle wall is the best-preserved part of the monastic church, and is one of the few places where the original ashlar stone facing and some of the decorative details still survive. The main building stone is a type of limestone which was imported from Caen in France. You can see the arches of the round-headed windows and a number of doorways, most of which have subsequently been blocked. One of these would have been the door for the monks to enter the church in procession from the cloister.

The stone vaults of the nave aisles were supported on stone arches and piers. The higher central part of the nave had a gallery which was lit by high-level windows in the outer walls. Above this was a third stage or clerestory.

Marked out on the ground of the nave is the plan of the earlier Anglo-Saxon churches. The remains of these lie about one metre below the floor of the Norman church (see page 25).

Now walk down the south aisle of the nave (to your right) towards the site of the rood screen. This was located between the second piers from the east end of the nave.

Before you reach this point, look at the foundations outside the south side of the nave to your right. These are the remains of two small buildings. The westernmost one, which is roughly square, was probably used as a temporary workshop during the demolition of the Abbey. The one to the east was a chapel possibly dedicated to St Mary, which was used for burials. You can still see two stone coffin-lids just outside this chapel.

On your left you can also see the remains of some floor tiles. These are some of the few tiles visible in their original position. They give an indication of how the floor may have looked in the late thirteenth century.

In the south aisle you also pass the site of the grave of Wulfmaeg, sister of Abbot Wulfric II, and the location of the Anglo-Saxon porticus of St Martin.

Glazed ceramic tile from a sixteenth-century tile pattern at St Augustine's showing daisies in circles and winged monsters

BELOW: *A reconstruction drawing of the nave of the Abbey church at its height, looking east towards the choir (drawing by Peter Urmston)*

THE ROOD SCREEN AND PULPITUM

The rood screen would have been made of intricately-carved wood on a stone base. It probably extended across the aisles to provide a barrier between the nave and the monks' choir and presbytery.

In front of the screen were several altars: in the centre the altar of the Holy Cross, in the south aisle an altar dedicated to the Annunciation of Our Lady, and in the north aisle a Lady Chapel of the late thirteenth century.

The area in front of the rood screen was a popular place for burial, and several thirteenth- and fourteenth-century abbots were buried here.

The area beyond the rood screen was reserved for the monks. Another screen made of stone (the pulpitum) separated the monks' choir from the rest of the church. The rood screen, pulpitum and monks' choir were in the area above the remains of Wulfric's Rotunda (see page 24), which would not have been visible in the later medieval period.

ST ANNE'S CHAPEL

To your right as you walk past the site of the pulpitum is the small chantry chapel of St Anne, used for saying Masses for the dead, which was added to the church in 1362 by Juliana de Leybourne, Countess of Huntingdon. The chapel contained a number of graves, including the tomb of Juliana herself who died in 1367.

Many fragments of carved and painted stonework were recovered from excavations in this area. Some are on display in the museum. The chapel must have been elaborately decorated with stone-painted panels and niches for statues of saints. Some of the stonework can still be seen *in situ* near where the altar would have been in the far left-hand corner of this chapel.

SOUTH TRANSEPT

In front of you lie the remains of the south transept which was built before 1087 during the abbacy of Abbot Scolland.

Soon after its completion the remains of several Anglo-Saxon kings were reburied here; the positions of the graves are marked by the modern tombs along the south wall. The kings

were originally buried in the Anglo-Saxon chapel of St Mary (see page 25), but were moved when the crypt was built during the 1070s. The tombs belong to Edbald (d.640), Lothaire (d.685), and Wihtred (d.725), all kings of Kent, and Mulus, King of Wessex, who was killed in a raid on Kent in 686. The other graves probably belong to King Erconbert (d.664), Abbot Roger of Chichester (d.1273) and Abbot Thomas Pouncy (d.1343).

In the east wall of the south transept is an apsidal chapel, dedicated to St John the Baptist.

In the north corner next to the altar is the base of a stone spiral stair which probably provided access to the central tower. Next to this was a further altar, dedicated to St Katherine, and a free-standing cross possibly near the steps leading to the crypt.

During the fourteenth century the south transept was re-roofed and possibly vaulted in stone. Some of the decorative stonework from this phase can be seen in the museum.

THE MONKS' CHOIR

The south transept and south aisle of the nave were separated from the monks' choir by a stone wall located between the crossing piers. The path goes through a modern gap in this wall.

The remains of some elaborate stone-carving in the far left-hand corner of St Anne's Chapel

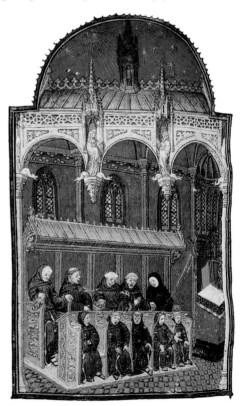

The monks' choir would have been located below the central tower on a raised platform behind the pulpitum, which divided it from the rest of the church. There would have been two rows of wooden choir stalls along each side wall and each monk would have had his own place in which to pray. From here the monks could look up to the high altar, with a screen behind it, and possibly glimpse the shrine of St Augustine beyond.

The choir was at the heart of monastic life, and would have been in almost constant use. Many of the services were sung or chanted, with some of the music being written by talented monks of the abbey such as John Dygon II, nephew to the abbot of the same name.

Very little can now be seen of the choir, as its remains were largely removed when Wulfric's Rotunda was excavated in 1914. However, you can still see evidence for the changes in level in this part of the church: the remains of the original Romanesque column bases on the west side of the piers are at a lower level than those in the centre.

Enamelled copper alloy disc found at St Augustine's — probably dating from the tenth century and thought to be the mount from a ring

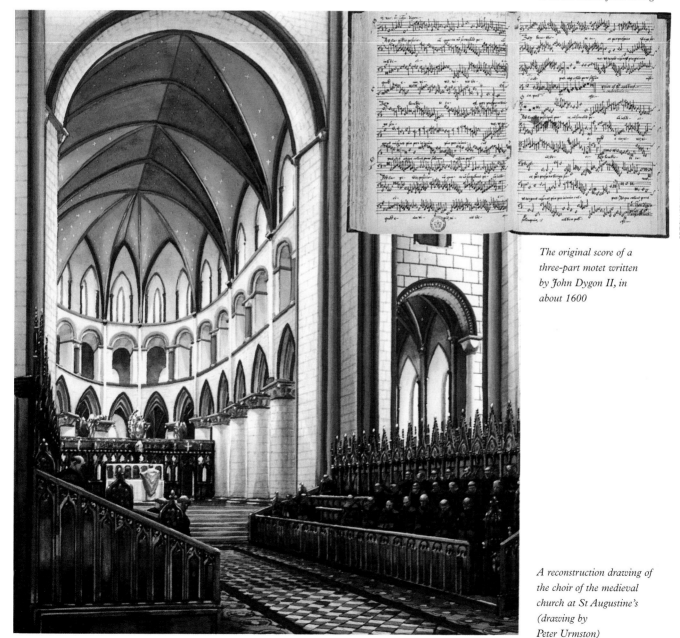

The original score of a three-part motet written by John Dygon II, in about 1600

A reconstruction drawing of the choir of the medieval church at St Augustine's (drawing by Peter Urmston)

The Norman crypt and the altar of the Chapel of St Mary and the Angels

Some decorative floor tiles, relaid from elsewhere in the church, can be seen on your left as you enter the Chapel of St Mary and the Angels

THE NORMAN CRYPT AND PRESBYTERY

From the corner of the south transept you can either go down the steps into the crypt or view it from ground level. The modern timber steps are in the same position as the medieval stone ones would have been.

The Norman crypt was the first part of the new church to be completed. It was in the Romanesque style (imitating the architecture of Ancient Rome) and was intended to be used for worship as well as for burials.

It lies on the site of the Anglo-Saxon church of St Mary which had to be cleared of all its burials before work on the new church could begin (see page 25).

As you go down the steps you are following in the footsteps of the medieval monks who would have walked in procession around the ambulatory (an area designed for this purpose).

The lower parts of the walls are still fairly well preserved and the ashlar stone facing blocks still have fine examples of the medieval masons' tooling marks.

As you go round the ambulatory you can see three chapels. On the right-hand (south) side is the chapel dedicated to St Thomas the Apostle. This is the best preserved chapel in the crypt, and you can still see the remains of the altar slab, which was found loose when the chapel was excavated, and probably originally came from the main church above. There are also

two corbel brackets made from Purbeck marble which may once have held small statues, and two cupboard recesses. Most of the floor tiles date from the thirteenth century.

The central chapel at the east end of the church was dedicated to The Blessed Virgin Mary in the Crypt. It was used for the singing of Mass each day until Abbot Thorne (1272–83) decided it should be sung in the new Lady Chapel in the nave instead, presumably so that the lay people could participate.

In 1325 the altar in this chapel was rededicated to St Mary and the Angels, and the alterations to the structure were possibly carried out at this time. The chapel was rebuilt with a square eastern end and the walls were plastered and painted. Low down on the wall to your left as you enter the chapel, some wall painting survives with a design of heraldic lions in circles. The altar itself was painted with red vertical bands. You can also see the remains of some decorative floor tiles, which seem to have been relaid here from elsewhere in the church.

Wall painting in the chapel of St Mary and the Angels. The design is of heraldic lions in circles

The modern roof was built over the chapel in 1937. At the same time the altar was reconstructed and rededicated so that the clergy of St Augustine's Missionary College could use it for Holy Communion. This altar is still occasionally used for services.

The northern chapel is not so well preserved, although part of the altar can still be seen. Abbot Wydo (1087–99) was buried here. It was dedicated to St Richard of Chichester during the second part of the thirteeth century.

The crypt, although partially below ground level, was well lit with five fifteenth-century windows on each side. The crypt had stone vaulting supported on columns, two of which you can still see. It is likely that these were reused from an earlier building of Anglo-Saxon or even Roman date. Abbot Scolland was buried in the centre of the crypt and a former abbot, Wulfric I (who died in 1006), was reburied beside him.

Above the crypt, and reflecting its shape, was the area of the presbytery. After walking round the crypt, return to ground level.

THE PRESBYTERY

The presbytery was the area immediately in front of the high altar. It was enclosed by thirteen columns, and had the main shrines of the Abbey behind it. These were reached by an ambulatory as in the crypt below. In the three chapels and the walls of the ambulatory were thirteen shrines containing the bones of eleven archbishops and of Abbot Hadrian and St Mildred (whose body had been brought from Minster in Thanet in 1030). These had all been ceremonially transferred to the new church from their original burial places in the nearby Saxon church of St Peter and St Paul (see page 25), in 1091. The shrine of St Augustine was in the central chapel.

The high altar and the shrines were on a higher level than the rest of the church, and must have been reached by a number of steps leading from the monks' choir. This concentrated attention on them as the monks progressed from west to east along the church.

A reliquary, holding the relics of St Ethelbert, stood on a shelf above the altar, flanked by books sent by Pope Gregory to Augustine for use by the English mission.

THE NORTH TRANSEPT

As you ascend the steps from the crypt you enter the north transept of the Norman church. The general layout reflects that of the south transept, but it was used in a slightly different way. To your left as you reach the top of the steps are the remains of a cupboard or small room, floored with glazed tiles, which was probably used by the Sacrist who was responsible for the maintenance of the church. The north transept had two altars. This area was used both by the monks who did not have

a stall in the choir, and by novices and those who had spent time in the infirmary.

In the north-east corner of the north transept, close to the modern access ramp, are the remains of a staircase that led down into the treasury or vestry. This was where many of the items used for church services were kept. In the north-west corner is the site of the grave of Abbot Dunster (d.1497).

The monks would have entered the church from the cloister into the eastern two bays of the nave. Next to the wall of the choir is a pit in which some weights, possibly from a clock or candelabrum, were found.

From here you can either go down the steps to look at the domestic buildings of the medieval abbey or continue to explore the story of the earlier churches on this site. If you decide to continue looking at the churches, return to the area of the medieval choir.

The medieval seal of St Augustine's Abbey

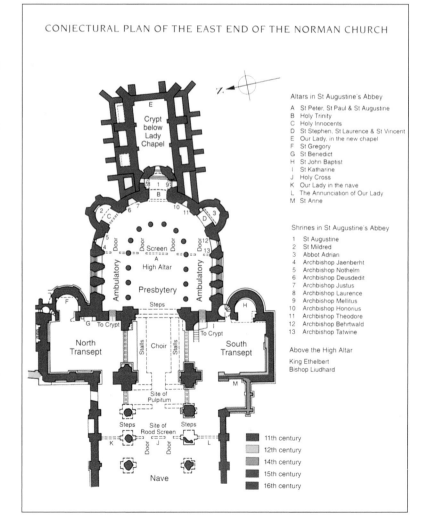

CONJECTURAL PLAN OF THE EAST END OF THE NORMAN CHURCH

E
Crypt below Lady Chapel

Screen
A
High Altar

Presbytery

Steps

To Crypt
To Crypt

North Transept
Choir
South Transept

Site of Pulpitum

Steps
Steps

Site of Rood Screen

Door
Door

Nave

Altars in St Augustine's Abbey
A St Peter, St Paul & St Augustine
B Holy Trinity
C Holy Innocents
D St Stephen, St Laurence & St Vincent
E Our Lady, in the new chapel
F St Gregory
G St Benedict
H St John Baptist
I St Katharine
J Holy Cross
K Our Lady in the nave
L The Annunciation of Our Lady
M St Anne

Shrines in St Augustine's Abbey
1 St Augustine
2 St Mildred
3 Abbot Adrian
4 Archbishop Jaenberht
5 Archbishop Nothelm
6 Archbishop Deusdedit
7 Archbishop Justus
8 Archbishop Laurence
9 Archbishop Mellitus
10 Archbishop Honorius
11 Archbishop Theodore
12 Archbishop Behrtwald
13 Archbishop Tatwine

Above the High Altar
King Ethelbert
Bishop Liudhard

11th century
12th century
14th century
15th century
16th century

THE ANGLO-SAXON MONASTERY

ABOVE: *Reconstruction drawings of the early, separate Anglo-Saxon churches (above) and the site during the mid-eleventh century (below) (drawings by Peter Urmston)*

Below the ruins of the medieval abbey are the remains of the earlier Anglo-Saxon monastery established by Augustine. They are about one metre (three feet) below the present ground surface. Following excavation they have largely been covered over, both for their long-term preservation and so that the later buildings can be more easily understood. Only the remains of Wulfric's Rotunda and part of the Porticus of St Gregory have been left exposed.

The location of the main walls of the early churches has been marked out in modern materials on the grass, and the plans in this guidebook will help you work out where they once stood.

The early monastery consisted of four separate churches or chapels, built in an east-west line across the site (see plan on back cover fold-out). The main church was dedicated to St Peter and St Paul, with the chapel of St Mary to the east and the church of St Pancras detached from the rest of the buildings, further towards the eastern boundary. To the west of St Peter and St Paul was a further small chapel.

Though no remains have been found, it is likely that there were also domestic quarters for the monks, probably built of timber.

Excavations below the medieval cloister revealed the remains of an earlier formal layout which probably dates to the period of Abbot Aelfmaer (1006–17).

ABBOT WULFRIC'S ROTUNDA

This is the remains of a crypt to an octagonal tower built by Abbot Wulfric in about 1050 to provide a link between the church of St Peter and St Paul, and the chapel of St Mary. It would have been entirely buried from sight when the Norman church was built, and has only been uncovered by archaeological excavation.

The crypt of the central tower of Abbot Wulfric's Rotunda as you see it today, built in about 1050. It was discovered in 1914 beneath the choir area of the later abbey church

The tower seems to have been designed as a four-storey galleried structure with a crypt, built around a central rotunda probably open from ground level to the roof. Columns for the roof of the central tower would have been supported on the wedge-shaped piers that you can still see. Abbot Wulfric was probably inspired by similar structures he had seen in France on his visit to Rheims. It seems likely that the tower was never completed, as Abbot Wulfric died in 1059, and his successor Abbot Scolland then replanned the entire church.

ST MARY'S CHURCH

Immediately in front of the information panel you can see the remains of a wall foundation made from reused Roman bricks, and held together with a pink mortar. This is all that now remains of the church of St Mary, which dates from about 620. The rest of this chapel was destroyed when Abbot Scolland built the Norman crypt. It is recorded by Goscelin, a chronicler of the Abbey in the late eleventh century, that the burials and relics from this chapel were collected and stored in the western tower, before being reburied when the new buildings were completed.

CHURCH OF ST PETER AND ST PAUL

This was the main church of the Saxon monastery, the construction of which was started during Augustine's lifetime, although it was completed by his successor, Archbishop Laurence, probably in about 613. It became the burial place of the early archbishops of Canterbury and the kings of Kent.

This first church was built from reused Roman bricks and originally consisted of a simple rectangular nave with a narthex or porch at the west end and side chapels known as porticus on the north and south. These side chapels were used for burials, as it was not customary to bury people in the main body of churches at this time. The east end was destroyed by the building of Wulfric's Rotunda, but studies of other churches of this date such as Reculver indicate that it would have had an eastern apse (curved end).

The stonework that you can see under the modern cover building is the external wall of the Porticus of St Gregory, and the remains of some of the tombs of the early archbishops who were buried here. These tombs were empty when discovered, as the remains of the bodies had been removed to the presbytery of the new Norman church in 1091. Originally they contained the remains of Archbishops Laurence (d.619), Mellitus (d.624) and Justus (d.634). The original graves of Augustine, Honorius and Deusdedit, now obscured by the later north nave wall, were also in this area.

The corresponding chapel on the south side of the nave, the Porticus of St Martin, now no longer visible, contained the remains of the early royal families of Kent, including King Ethelbert and his wife Bertha.

Once these chapels became filled with burials, further burials were placed in the nave. These included Abbot Hadrian and St Mildred before the high altar, as well as Archbishops Theodore and Berhtwald.

During the tenth century, probably under the direction of Archbishop Dunstan (959–88), the church was again extended further to the west and rededicated in 978 to include the name of St Augustine. Further towards the west end of the medieval nave another chapel, together with the foundations of a freestanding square tower, was uncovered during the excavations of the area in the 1950s. It is likely that these date from the early eleventh century.

The fourth Anglo-Saxon church, dedicated to St Pancras, is described on page 30.

ABOVE: *Mosaic decoration from the early twentieth century in the Chapel of St Gregory and St Augustine, Westminster Cathedral. This shows a procession of St Augustine and monks carrying an icon arriving before King Ethelbert and Queen Bertha*

The modern covered area containing the burial sites of several of the early archbishops and the external wall of the Porticus of St Gregory

THE CLOISTER
and
MONASTIC BUILDINGS

Y ou will now step forward again in time to the Middle Ages, to tour the cloister and domestic buildings. The remains of these can be seen from the north transept, and you can enter the cloister down the stone steps by which the monks would have entered the church. Unlike most Benedictine abbeys, the domestic buildings of St Augustine's were on the north side of the church, probably in order to avoid the cemetery to the south.

THE CLOISTER

The cloister was laid out as part of Abbot Scolland's total replanning of the Abbey in the 1070s, although most of the construction of the domestic buildings was probably carried out during the abbacy of Hugh of Fleury (1099–1124). The cloister reached its final form under Abbot Thorne in 1276.

It is roughly square, 37m x 35m (122 x 117 feet), and comprised a garth or garden, surrounded by covered alleys enclosed by an open or partially-glazed arcade.

Although the monks spent a considerable amount of time praying and performing services in the church, the rest of their day would have been spent around the cloister. It formed the main living area, and gave access to all the main buildings of the Abbey.

The cloister area showing the various recesses and doorways in the west wall

THE SOUTH ALLEY

As you come down the steps into the cloister, turn left into the south alley, which would have been used for reading and meditation. Towards the western end was the school where the novices were taught. You can still see the alcove next to the church door where the books were kept. The novices would have been supervised by the Precentor and his assistant the Succentor who had seats nearby. The monks would have sat to read or copy manuscripts in study cubicles or carrels attached to the arcade. Towards the far end is a blocked doorway which was once a processional entrance into the nave of the church.

THE WEST ALLEY AND WEST RANGE

As you turn right at the corner into the west cloister alley there is an elaborate doorway which led into the buildings of the west range. Originally these included the outer parlour where the monks could have held conversations with external visitors, and the office and storeroom of the Cellarer, the monastic official in charge of the Abbey's estates and provisions. On the first floor above these rooms was probably the guesthouse.

In the late thirteenth century the whole of this range was remodelled to form the Abbot's lodging. The outer parlour became the Abbot's parlour with his personal chapel above; the main accommodation was at first-floor level, including an office for his chaplain. These apartments included a chamber and a great hall, which was located at the north end of the range where the school library, built by William Butterfield, is now. The cloister prior would have supervised activity in the cloister from his seat near the central doorway.

The Cellarer's quarters were rebuilt on the north side of the Great Court in the later thirteenth century, and the guest range was moved to the west side along what is now Monastery Street.

The blocked doorway to the original west range

LEFT: *Alcove in the south alley of the cloister near to the church door. Used to store books*

THE RULE OF ST BENEDICT
AND THE BENEDICTINE ORDER

The Rule of St Benedict

Monasticism had its origins in third-century Egypt, when a number of Christians decided to dedicate themselves to a solitary life of meditation, prayer and self-mortification. The word monk comes from the Greek *monos* meaning alone.

Some of these early hermits gradually organised into groups, and found benefits from living as part of a religious community. Monasticism gradually spread to Europe, and some of the early ideas were written down to form a series of rules for the monastic way of life.

The most influential of these was the Rule written by St Benedict, an Italian monk who founded the abbey of Monte Cassino near Naples in the early sixth century. Benedict saw the monastery as a self-sufficient unit, and encouraged the monks to have minimum contact with the outside world. His rule laid out a code of conduct for leading an ordered way of life based on the teachings of the Gospels, and proposed a timetable for religious observance and other activities.

The most important part of the monks' life was to carry out the *Opus Dei* (the work of God) by performing eight liturgical services, which became known as the canonical hours.

Many early monasteries, including that of St Andrew's on the Caelian Hill in Rome, where Augustine was the Prior, followed these basic principles, and it seems likely that the early Saxon monastery of St Peter and St Paul in Canterbury was organised on these lines.

In this period the idea of a formal and distinct religious order was unknown, and monasteries were all organised as individual units. Each monastery was headed by an abbot to whom the monks swore a vow of obedience.

The idea of distinct religious orders was developed during the tenth century by the abbey of Cluny in France. When new monasteries were founded by monks from Cluny, they were an extension of the original community, rather than independent houses. Each monk in the new foundations swore their vow of obedience to the Abbot of Cluny, and not to the head of the new monastery. This idea of monasteries being part of an extended family developed throughout the early medieval period, and by the thirteenth century a considerable number of religious orders, with distinct variations in religious practice, could be recognised.

Benedictine houses in England were usually among the earlier foundations, with their origins in the Saxon period, and were reorganised during the reforms of Archbishop Dunstan (959–88). They were often wealthy, well-endowed monasteries with royal connections like St Augustine's, and included those English cathedrals which were run on monastic lines such as Christ Church in Canterbury. The monks were distinguishable from monks of other orders by their black robes or habits.

NORTH ALLEY AND NORTH RANGE

When you reach the end of the west alley, turn right again into the north alley of the cloister.

This led to the monks' dining hall or refectory. Immediately outside the door in the north-west corner of the cloister are two decorative recesses which were possibly for storing items associated with the refectory. You can also see blocked arches along this wall which may be the remains of an ornamental arcade. The senior monks would have had seats along this, the sunny side of the cloister.

The monks would wash before entering the refectory. The hexagonal foundation within the cloister garth was part of a freestanding lavatorium or washing place with a water tower above, built in about 1270. This would have been fed by piped water from the abbey conduit house on St Martin's Hill to the east of the site. The Conduit House is in the care of English Heritage, and can still be visited.

Two decorative recesses situated in the north alley of the cloister and possibly used for storing items associated with the refectory

THE REFECTORY

The entrance to the refectory led into a cross-passage with an internal door into the dining hall, and another door leading out to the kitchen at the far end. This building was rebuilt in the 1260s under Abbot Roger II.

At the east end of the refectory was a dais or raised platform on which the Abbot's table would have been placed. An early excavation photograph shows evidence of an undercroft below floor level which was possibly used for storage. You can still see the remains of arches on the north side of the building, which gave access to the undercroft from the kitchen.

All meals would have been taken communally in the refectory. There was a rule of silence, with the monks communicating in sign language if strictly necessary, while one of the monks read a lesson from the Bible.

THE KITCHEN

Beyond the refectory, to the north, was a freestanding hexagonal kitchen. It was built in about 1290 during the abbacy of Abbot Fyndon, and probably replaced an earlier kitchen. Kitchen buildings were often built slightly apart from the other buildings in order to minimise the risk of fire. There were probably four hearths and two entrances, one into the refectory, the other leading to the outer court where the supplies would have been delivered. The roof was steeply pitched and made of lead with louvres to let the smoke out. This building survived until after the dissolution of the monastery, and continued to be used as the kitchen for the royal palace.

THE MONKS' DORMITORY

To the east of the kitchen and refectory are the remains of the monks' dormitory, which was a large two-storey building with an aisle on the east side. Only two buttresses and a single gable of this building survive. The monks would have slept on the upper floor, which would probably have had direct access to the reredorter or latrine. This has never been excavated, but probably lay at right-angles to the dormitory in the area of the present field boundary. The ground floor of the dormitory may have been used, among other things, as a monks' parlour where conversation would be allowed at certain times. The dormitory is unusual in that it seems never to have had a separate stair leading directly to the church for the monks to use for night services. It did have direct access into the passage leading to the infirmary. It was here that the bench end which you can see in the museum was found.

THE INFIRMARY

Under what is now the school playing field lie the foundations of the monastic infirmary and associated buildings. Here, sick and elderly monks and some local benefactors were cared for. The area was excavated between 1902 and 1912, but was covered over again. In dry weather it is sometimes possible to see the location of the buried walls showing as parch-marks in the grass.

Beyond the infirmary complex were the gardens of the Cellarer, and probably the Abbot.

THE EAST ALLEY

Now return to the cloister down the modern flight of steps. Close to this point was the prior's seat, which was opposite the door to the inner parlour and the passage to the infirmary. Next to this would have been the stairs leading up to the dormitory. The east alley was often also used for burials.

THE CHAPTER HOUSE

The next doorway that you come to led into the chapter house. This was used for the daily meeting of the monastic community where major decisions about the running of the Abbey were made. The chapter house got its name from the fact that a chapter from the Rule of St Benedict was read here each day. It was also a favoured place for the burial of Abbots; eight are known to have been buried here.

An aerial photograph of the infirmary area. It is now hidden under the school playing field, but some outlines can be seen from the air when there are drought conditions

A boss from the intersection of ribs in the vaulted ceiling of the chapter house rebuilt in the 1380s

The chapter house was first built in about 1100, but was rebuilt between 1324 and 1332, and then repaired following damage by an earthquake in 1382. It was a rectangular building with a stone vaulted roof and elaborate internal decoration. Around three of the walls was a stone bench with individual seats for the monks defined by a carved stone canopy above with painted leaves and stone heads. The abbot would have had his throne in the centre of the east wall, flanked by seats for the prior and sub-prior.

Now return to the north transept of the abbey church by the semi-circular steps. To your left, near the base of these, is a Purbeck marble base which is all that remains of a thirteenth-century lavatorium or washing-place.

The tour continues by the modern access ramp which takes you round the outside of the church. This ramp lies over the space between the chapter house and the church which was used as the treasury, and for security reasons was not directly accessible from the cloister. It may have had an upper storey for the storage of books and important abbey documents. Although this abbey was noted for its production of illuminated manuscripts, the location of the scriptorium has not been identified, though it may have been above the east alley of the cloister.

The access ramp leads you into the area which was the monks' cemetery, between the church and the infirmary.

A small fragment of carved stone foliage from a canopy above one of the monk's seats in the late fourteenth-century chapter house

Abbot Simon of St Albans reading next to a book chest. From a fourteenth-century illustration

BRITISH LIBRARY Cotton Claudius EIV f124

THE LADY CHAPEL

In front of you now lie the remains of the Lady Chapel. Lady chapels were common in the fifteenth century and were used for special performances of Masses and antiphons (religious pieces where two groups of voices sing or chant alternately).

All that is left now is a rather confusing set of foundations, with low-level walls, which originally formed part of a crypt chapel. In fact, what you see are the remains of two separate buildings of slightly different dates.

The earlier, outer, foundations, probably dating from the early fifteenth century, are made of flint and stone and formed a chapel of five bays with external buttresses. The creation of this must have involved moving the shrine of St Augustine, which was still situated in the central apsidal chapel behind the high altar in 1414.

It is not certain whether this building was ever completed, but it was taken down and rebuilt, presumably during the time of Abbot Dygon (1497–1509), whose tomb was found in a small crypt chamber in this new chapel.

The new chapel was smaller and simpler in plan than the first one on this site. It was almost certainly built by Robert Vertue, who was probably the master mason at St Augustine's Abbey at this time.

Beyond the Lady Chapel are the remains of a wall, probably eleventh-century, which originally divided the monks' cemetery from the lay cemetery to the south. Follow this wall until you reach the last building of the Abbey on this tour.

CHAPEL OF ST PANCRAS

This was the easternmost of the line of churches built during the Anglo-Saxon period, and is the only one of which substantial remains can still be seen. It has survived because its position did not interfere with the Norman rebuilding of the Abbey church. It continued in use as a cemetery chapel, and contains a number of burials.

The Anglo-Saxon parts of the building can be distinguished from the phases of later rebuilding by the exclusive use of reused Roman brick. This is similar to the technique of building found in the buried remains of the church of St Peter and St Paul. It is likely to have been built during the seventh century, although in the fourteenth century the monks believed that this was an earlier pagan building which had been consecrated and used by

The remains of the Chapel of St Pancras at the far east end of the site

A Roman column reused in the building of St Pancras' Chapel

St Augustine. It was believed that Augustine had said his first Mass in Canterbury in the area of the southern chapel.

The original building consisted of a nave with an apsidal chancel at the east end, and small single chapels on the north and south sides. The nave was divided from the chancel by a screen supported on four columns, one of which you can still see. The altar would have been situated at the east end.

The building seems to have been rebuilt during the middle years of the eighth century, largely to the same plan, but with the addition of a porch at the west end.

In 1361 the chancel of the chapel was damaged in a storm, and was rebuilt with a square east end. The window which now dominates this end of the building was probably inserted into the wall in about 1390. In 1494 it was recorded that a hermit lived here.

This is the last building on the tour, and you can now either return directly to the museum, or follow the path to the top of the mound to your right.

THE CAMPANILE MOUND

This mound has recently been modified to allow for disabled access and an audio-visual display which helps to explain the history of the Abbey, but it was a feature which would have been familiar to the monks of St Augustine's Abbey. On top of it was a bell tower or campanile – probably a timber structure sitting on stone foundation walls. We do not know when this was built. There is a fine aerial view of the Abbey ruins from here.

THE LAY CEMETERY

The area between the campanile mound and the museum was once the site of a public cemetery. A number of buildings originally stood in the cemetery, one of which was discovered during excavations just to the south of the monastic church. This building was probably the remains of the cemetery chapel which was consecrated in 1299. It had a crypt for the storage of bones and a chapel for saying Masses for the dead. Documents also suggest that there was a further water tower or conduit in this area, although no remains of this have been uncovered.

BRITISH LIBRARY Royal 18 d1 f148

Canterbury pilgrims

EXCAVATIONS AT THE ABBEY

archaeological interest in the site of St Augustine's Abbey began in 1844 when A. J. Beresford Hope bought the site to build a missionary college.

Hope saw the College as having a "double character": to educate missionaries, and to preserve, excavate and display the site to the public. The College wardens set up a series of appeals for funding, and Hope himself bought land within the precinct whenever it came up for sale.

The first archaeological excavation on the site was carried out soon afterwards by William Butterfield, before building the College library. Many decorative medieval floor tiles were found and some of the designs were reproduced by Mintons.

Students of the College undertook a number of excavations during the later part of the nineteenth century in the area of the kitchen, refectory and cloister. In most cases this was a simple clearance exercise. There were some interesting finds but it is not always clear exactly where they came from or how old they were.

In 1900 Canon Routledge, who had already made a study of St Martin's Church, was keen to excavate the Abbey church, and a committee was set up to raise the money and to advise. This committee included the eminent antiquarian St John Hope. Excavations started towards the eastern part of the site with the church of St Pancras and the Lady Chapel and the Norman crypt.

After the death of Routledge in 1904, the excavations lost impetus, and it was not until the appointment of Robert Potts as the sub-warden in 1912 that excavations in the nave were resumed. Problems involving the mortuary and laundry of the County Hospital, which covered the south transept, were eventually overcome.

Perhaps some of the most exciting discoveries were unearthed in 1914–15, when the first evidence for the Saxon churches was revealed. Excavations continued intermittently throughout the

Early twentieth-century excavations clearance at St Augustine's

1920s to uncover the buildings around the cloister, and in 1934 the first plan of the whole excavated site was published.

In 1937 the hospital moved to a new site, and plans to demolish the buildings and turn the area into a public garden were proposed. In the event, the land was bought by a new body of trustees (the St Augustine's Abbey Precinct Recovery Fund), and the hospital buildings were leased for a period of twenty-one years to the City Council for use as a technical college, on the understanding that at the end of this time the site would be used as a garden. This plan was finally realised in 1971, the hospital buildings were demolished, and further excavations took place to the south of the monastic church, before the garden was opened in 1977.

The northern part of the site was sold for the building of a teacher training college (Christ Church College) in 1961, although no archaeological work was carried out at this time. The first excavations in this area took place in 1983, and have continued intermittently since. A complex sequence of archaeological layers dating from the present day back to the Neolithic period have been uncovered.

Remains of the Cellarer's range and the brewhouse and bakehouse complex have been found. These were built in the late thirteenth or early fourteenth century when the area became part of the Outer Court of the Abbey. Before this date the area was used for both agricultural and industrial purposes. Substantial numbers of finds dating from the eighth and ninth centuries suggest that this may have been a secular settlement which grew up to the north of the monastery. Many of the finds from the excavations are now on display in the new site museum.

The tomb of Abbot Roger II (1252–72) as found in the south transept of the Abbey church during excavations in 1918

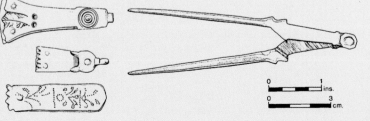

Items found at the Abbey site in 1960, probably from the scriptorium. Left to right: strip of book binding; pair of tweezers; book clasps and a small pair of compasses with copper alloy arms